Dedicated to my husband, the love of my life. And to my two children, Ella and Winston, who taught me that motherhood could be everything I thought it couldn't be. I love you all to the stars and back again.

DINOSAUR
HOUSE
We Turn Industry Leaders into Kids Book Authors

www.DinosaurHouse.com

MOMMY LOVES YOU WHEN

You know **MOMMY LOVES YOU**, RIGHT?

MOMMY LOVES YOU WHEN YOU'RE **HAPPY** AND **EXCITED** AND **SMILEY**

...AND MOMMY LOVES YOU WHEN YOU'RE **GRUMPY** OR **ANGRY** OR **SAD**.

THERE IS TRULY NOTHING ON **PLANET EARTH** THAT
COULD EVER MAKE MOMMY NOT LOVE YOU.

I LIKE WHO YOU ARE. I **LOVE** LISTENING TO THE THINGS THAT **YOU** HAVE TO SAY.

"This is you! And this is daddy!"

"And this is me! And this is a llama! The llama is our boss and our job is to make umbrellas!"

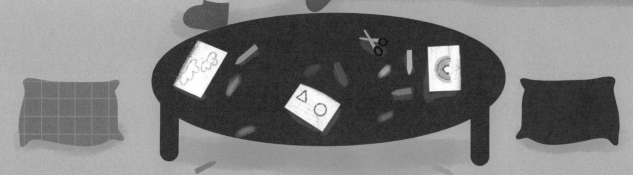

I LOVE SPENDING **TIME WITH YOU**.
I LOVE **BEING AROUND YOU**.

"This is the business building.
Time for business!"

...BECAUSE YOU'RE MINE AND I'M **SO PROUD** OF YOU.

TALK ABOUT IT

What are 3 things you love about
your mommy?

1. _____
2. _____
3. _____

What are 3 things your mommy loves
about you?

1. _____
2. _____
3. _____

DINOSAUR
HOUSE

We Turn Industry Leaders into Kids Book Authors

At Dinosaur House, we make the kind of books purpose-driven parents want to read to their kids.

Sign up to our newsletter and we'll send you a free copy of our next book:

SCAN ME

Made in United States
Troutdale, OR
11/20/2024

25104467R00019